Chip's 1, 2, 3

Written by Roderick Hunt

Illustrated by Alex Brychta

OXFORD
UNIVERSITY PRESS

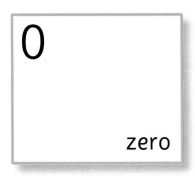

0

zero

Floppy has lost his bone.

He has nothing to chew, so there is nothing in the box.

Kipper only had one balloon.

Count one balloon in the box.

2
two

Kipper loves his toys.

Count the toys in the box.

Oh no! Look at poor old Dad.

Count the frogs in the box.

4 four

The children had a picnic.

Count the cups in the box.

five 5

Wilma has a little dog.

Count the dogs in the box.

6

six

Dad's trousers are tucked in his socks.

Count the socks in the box.

seven

7

Chip is learning about nature.

Count the plant pots in the box.

8 eight

Chip is dressing up.

Count the hats in the box.

nine

Wilf is not wearing his boots.

Count the boots in the box.

10 ten

Wilma likes to play football.

Count the balls in the box.

11

eleven

Chip needs some new shoes.

Count the shoes in the box.

12

twelve

It took ages to make this sandcastle.

Count the sandcastles in the box.

13

thirteen

Floppy has a starfish on his back.

Count the starfishes in the box.

14

fourteen

Oh no! Floppy has taken Dad's cake.

Count the cakes in the box.

15

fifteen

Dad has a surprise for Mum.

Count the presents in the box.

16 sixteen

Kipper has found an amazing shell.

Count the shells in the box.

17

seventeen

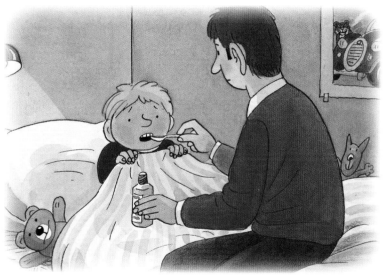

Dad gave Kipper some medicine.

Count the bottles in the box.

18 eighteen

Floppy loves to chase butterflies.

Count the butterflies in the box.

19
nineteen

Biff and Chip say fruit is good for you.

Count the fruits in the box.

Kipper likes to build models.

Count the bricks in the box.

Talk about numbers

See if you can count up to 20.

Count the different children in this book.

How old are you? What date is your birthday?

Look for the page numbers. Where are they?

Number grid

Shut your eyes then put your finger on the page.
Read the number in the square.

1	2	3
6	7	8
11	12	13
16	17	18

4	5
9	10
14	15
19	20

Odd one out

All the numbers appear three times.
But one number appears four times.
Which is it?

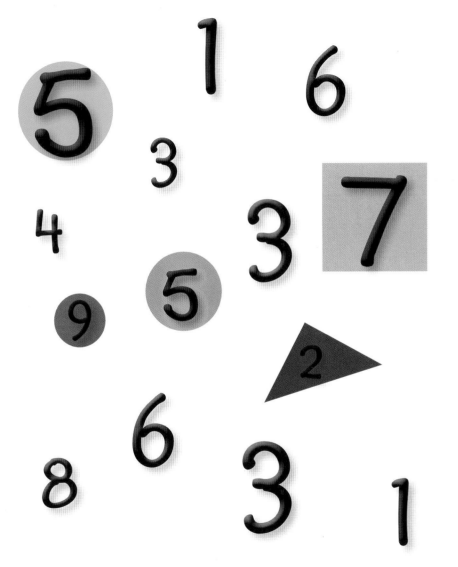

Find the pair

Two of these teapots are the same.
See if you can find them.

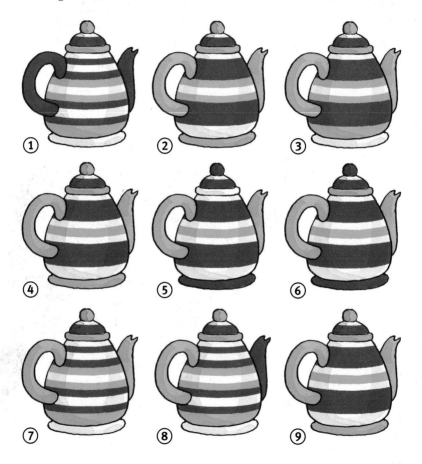